I think I can Fly

Kylie Webber

BookLeaf
Publishing

India | USA | UK

Presentation by *BookLeaf Publishing*

Web: www.bookleafpub.com

E-mail: info@bookleafpub.com

ISBN: 9789357616195

First edition 2023

I would like to dedicate this book to all who have crossed my path and inspired me to change. The friends that have come and gone and to the ones I still have.

Most of all I would like to dedicate this book to my daughter, for without her I would not be who I am today.

ACKNOWLEDGEMENT

I would like to Acknowledge Toni Gray- Super mum extraordinaire on the pathway to change.

I think i can fly

I think I can fly
i will give it a try.

A warm summer's day
and a clear blue sky.

I think I can fly
i will give it a try.

Observing the birds all flapping their wings
enjoying the freedom that flying does bring.

I think I can fly
i will give it a try.

Thinking and thinking how can it be so…
The landing the takeoff and how far will I go?

I think I can fly
I will give it a try.

I climb and climb to get to the top,
braver and braver climbing nonstop

I think I can fly
I will give it a try

Now balancing on a fence post so high
with tiny arms spread out so wide.

Calling out as loud as I could
"Come watch me mum, come have a look".

I think I can fly
i will give it a try.

Patient mum standing on the front porch,
Hands on hips and a smile on her lips.

"Go on then, if you think you can fly,
just give it a try".

Determined to make it a little further today
I bend my knees and I get set to play.

I think I can fly
I will give it a try

Flapping my arms just like the birds
I jump from the post whilst screaming the words

I'm flying, I'm flying, I'm flying so high.

The quick rush to the ground as I land with a
thud
A little further this time, my marker has judged.

Cheeks rosy red and a feeling of pride
I know I can fly
I just have to try.

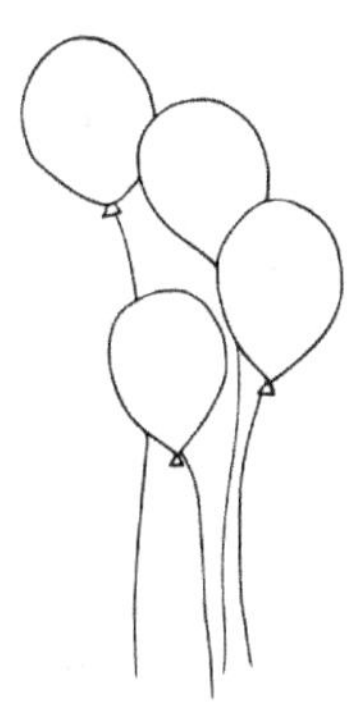

An artist- Age 8

When we are little.
they all want to know

What will we be when we are grown?

A firefighter, or nurse they question us intently
Perhaps looking for the answer that hinders them
so,
seeking inspiration for change if only they
could.
So lost in the land of adulthood,

The day had come and my dad asked me so
"what is it you want to be when you are grown?"

With a sense of excitement I loudly proclaimed

"An artist is what I want to be when I am
grown"

With his familiar smirk and his quick sense of
wit,

He asked me if a 'bullshit artist" is what I had
meant.

A strange sense of confusion reigned faint
No, I said I meant one that can paint.

Looking down to me, the words echoed loud.

An artist? And one that can paint, that could be
tough, do you think you're good enough?

Such silly words that never meant to hurt
Created such doubt as I wondered the earth.

Memories and imagination are created everyday
So I changed that scenario to all go my way

Now in my mind he has asked me again

"what is it you want to be when you are grown?"

With a sense of excitement I loudly proclaimed

"An artist is what I want to be when I am
grown"

Looking down to me, the words echo loud.

An artist? And one that can paint, that could be tough.

So let's buy you the things so you can learn because Kylie my child, to me you're good enough.

The night it happened

Watching you collapse to the floor,
hearing your scream so piercing.
As you were told.
A blood-curdling noise I will never forget

A quiet voice screams inside
please hold me, please love me I silently cried
confusion, anger, rejection.
I was an observer of heartbreak

Not understanding, but knowing.
Yet still the quiet voice screams inside
please hold me please love me

Shut out, shut down, feeling alone
total shock no breath just floating
I was an observer of heartbreak

Alcohol, tears, laughter
family felt like strangers.
I don't know why.
I was hiding, I wanted to scream
I was angry.
I was an observer of heartbreak.

The quiet voice remained for some time
But time has given me wisdom
And I understand why
You couldn't hold me
You couldn't love me
Because your heart was breaking.

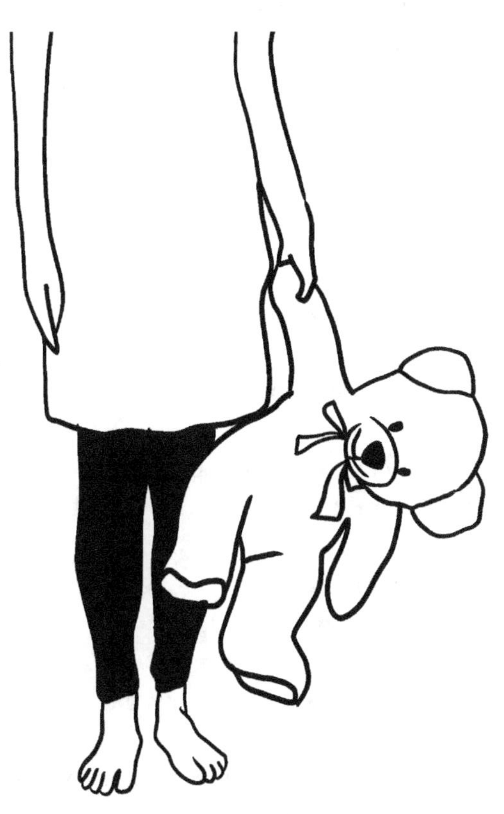

The years that followed

Ignoring the inner wisdom
Has its own consequences

The quiet voice had no confidence
It was smart, it was logical
But it was not verbal

I kept my emotions hidden
Avoiding connection
Could not voice my opinion
To scared of rejection

This led me to all sorts of beliefs
About the world, my self, never giving relief.

Then you came along
Promising the world
An escape from my mundane
But just really playing your own game

The one good thing to come from you was her,
So beautiful, so deserving of a love I could not
give.

Age 16

Ignoring the signs,
And lying to you
I knew deep down
I knew it was true

This is what happens
When the quiet voice remains.
A mind so fastened
That it cannot explain.

I knew I could not express reality
For fear of your shame and pending finality.

Then the day came
It could not be denied
I was sixteen
With a baby inside.

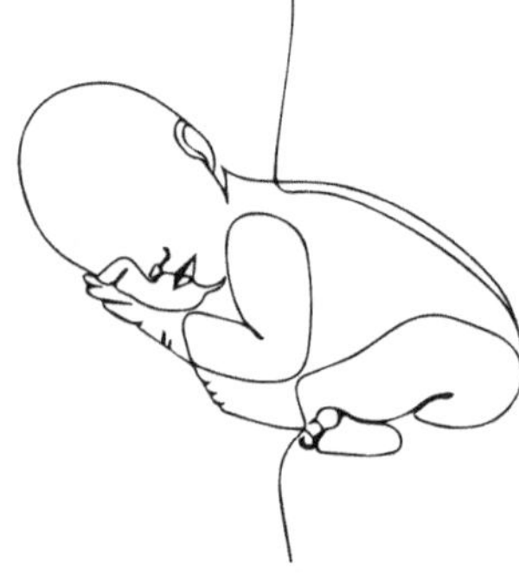

You

You, sweet precious innocent you.
Holding you for eternity.
Staring into you, wondering how could I do you
justice
Realising that I could not ever let go of all the
love a mother should give
For fear of the loss and the heartbreak of grief.

Not wanting to break you, nor leave you alone
I did my best and I loved you so
But it was hard having responsibility so young

Support came and went but in the end
It was just us two

Our bond is unique and special.

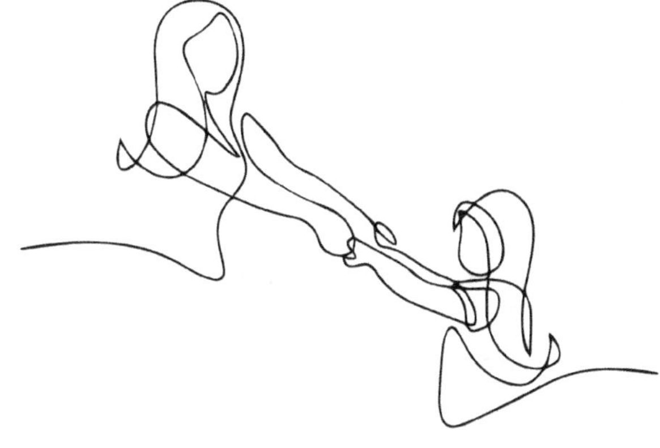

Playing House

I was a mum and you were a dad
Living the funniest life we thought we could
have

Loads of adventures and lots of potential
The choices we made never seemed
inconsequential

But oh how we were wrong
When we both heard that song!

Still growing up but beside each other
We fight, makeup and we recover.

You lead, I follow forsaking my time
Ignoring the stages of my own self decline

For the most part I think I am happy
But succumbing to numbness and letting it trap
me

So many moments, I should have just left
Learning and knowing about disrespect

One more move and one more chance
I could see our future mapped out like a dance

Finally I thought he would just pick me
And I could stop being what he wanted me to be

How was he to know if I could not clearly
explain
That I was sick of playing the stupid games

I did try to say 'I want this no more'
I don't care anymore was what I said
But who knows what the fuck you heard in your
head

A free ticket I guess was what you received
To egotistical and arrogant not thinking i'd leave

Leaving

As I sit and stare beyond my mirrored reflection
I believe I am there with deep introspection

A little girl trapped inside
A quiet voice remaining unheard

Well, no more, no more yells the silent scream
It turns into tears over forsaken shattered dreams

I felt like a little girl asking if I could leave,
begging you to let me go -
Not knowing what I would do if you said no.

My heart wide open, and private life on display
Began two years of my emotional disarray

Not living in the moment not taking control
It was just day by day, letting it all unfold

Acting without thinking, speaking without
thought
I was like a train of the rails no purpose was
sought

Collateral damage was in plain sight
But I couldn't see it, emotions shut tight

What had I done to my little family
I was struggling to face it and it was selfish of
me.

I did what I did, not really knowing why
Trying to get through, with lie after lie.

Making big promises I could not keep
I started a journey that made others weep

A big downward spiral was what it became
Different masks, different hats just to play the
game

It took me a while to rise up again
Some damage done, but hope remained.

A fun life

And so it began, a new journey a new life
So many firsts, I can not explain
A life with such freedom and a new sense of self
I felt like a top prize plucked from a shelf

Many weekends were spent
Where they shouldn't have been
Away from my nest
But still trying my best
To be there for you
guilt-ridden for not wanting to

A friendship broken

I was blind and yet I could see.
I could see the chaos I was creating in your life
yet I didn't have the strength needed for calm.

I was blind as I did not know how to ease your
emotions.

I was too scared to love you and connect with
you for fear of losing you. I knew what it meant
to lose precious adoring and admirable
unconditional love.

I did not know you would have felt scared,
alone, abandoned, uncared for, unloved,
frightened, isolated, lonely and sad, how could
I?

 I only saw hatred, anger, walls and
rebellion amidst the strength, willpower and
determination.

I was ignorant to the fact that you just needed
me to be there.

I saw your beauty and happiness when you let
me in.
I was too scared to grow up. I did not know what
that would mean. I was selfish, I was tired, I was
easily influenced, I was burdened by the weight
and responsibility of life. The emotions too
heavy to bear.

I lied thinking I was protecting you.

I lied to keep you happy.

I lied because I was hiding from you.

I lied to hide from reality.

My stomach was knotted with guilt.

I know my words haunt you and have hurt you.
You did not deserve the things I said.

I was angry that I did not do better.

I was angry that you were right.

I was angry that I was scared.

I was angry at me.

Through the passage of time I realised that I was living my life at the expense of your youth.

I did not realise that I would have had a best friend. The friendship that would have calmed the chaos.

I heard your advice, but did not heed the wisdom and maturity of the words spoken.

I broke your trust.

I invaded your private world.

Battle lines were drawn. These lines are imaginary. But perhaps now ingrained.

I miss you. I love you.

I grew up because you taught me how.

Twin flame journey

Is there really one

What I felt with you
I felt with no other

Connected by force
melding together

Was it as real for you
As it was real for me?

Twin flame journey

A purpose fulfilled

A void unfilled
A hollow heart

No direction, just coasting
Through a life torn apart

Is there a path
That we all must lead?

Or is it just by chance
How we mindlessly accede?

Why are we here and is there a right way
To live your life filling time til doomsday

Seeking and searching for that feeling of bliss
Fake filling the void with each choice amiss

A purpose fulfilled
Feels like nothing else

A wonderful moment
A body alive
A surge of energy
That started this ride

A sense of direction
Now fills the void

No more seeking or searching
For that feeling of bliss or false validation from
your sweet kiss

I had my self, I knew no other
That could make the decision
To be of service to others

Was fate a player in my journey ahead
Or destiny now the steps I must tread?

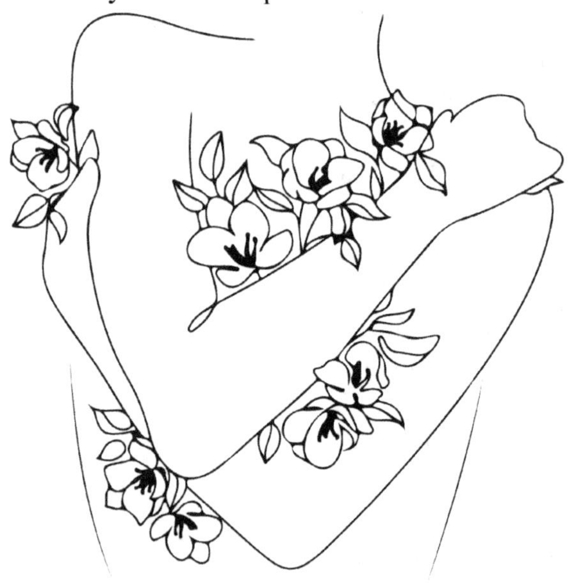

The consequences of
emotional unavailability.

Love found and love lost
Was what it had cost

Not trusting your mind, Nor trusting your heart
But dreaming a life you're too fragile to start.

Ignoring the voice with words left unspoken
To scared of the feelings abruptly awoken

Feeling uncomfortable and just pretending
Not knowing oneself true personality pending

A girl in a man's world- he acting the boy
Playing with things just like a toy

Was it him was it me? Did I get it all wrong
Giant walls -up for so long.

Why couldn't we be honest and clear
Was it real what I felt -did you even care?

Emotions don't lie and we feel them with force
Imagine those emotions not returned only on
show as trickery

Frustration and confusion
You became my obsession
Memories with questions
Every scene dissected
Reaching out but consistently rejected

Looking for meaning and a glimmer of hope
That I was the one to cut the heart's rope.

Two sides of a coin is what I could see one you one me,
Harbouring consequences of emotional unavailability.

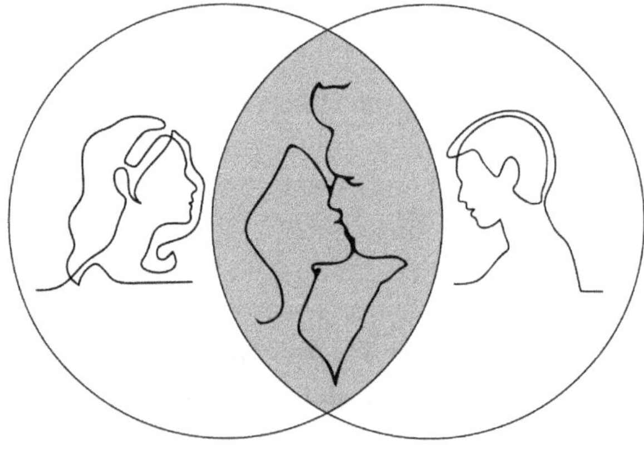

Accepting defeat

The memories that haunt me that should make
me happy
A flicker of a vision that breaks my soul.
Knowing the love I feel could not be expressed.
I can not connect.
I ponder Is to feel love also to be lost.
I Surrender

Riding it out

Garnering the strength to make a change
Know things again will never be the same
People, places all similar faces
Day in day out just riding the wave
Until the time that comes
When decisions are made
A life no longer stagnant

The game of life

Life can be cruel
Life can joy
Life can be games
Life can be messy
Life can be bleak
Life can be love
Life can be tough
Life can be fun
Life can be hard
Life can begin
Life can be easy
Life can be change

Life ends.

The choice was made it cannot be undone

I thought it was you
But it wasn't.
A beam of light through an open door.
A shadow of a guard on watch.

A body unfamiliar.

A mind unconscious but a split second of true
recognition.

Hidden under a mask for so long
The ice breaks and I remember

You don't know that I know.
But I do.

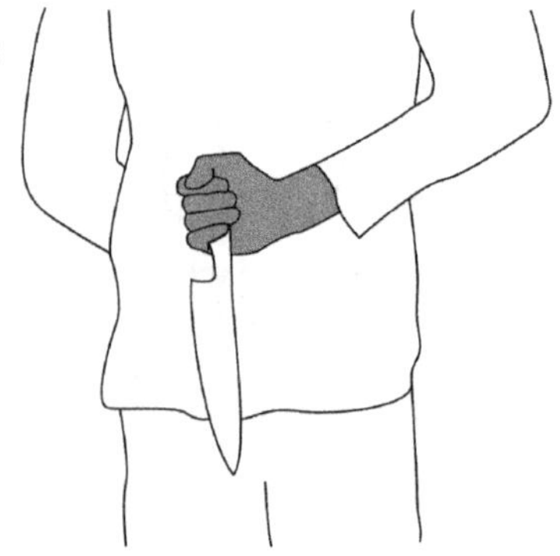

A joyful day

The sun is shining
The air is warm

The water is cool
The sand is hot

I like days like these
I like them a lot

A simple time to do as I please

A towel on the beach
A pleasant breeze

The simple things
So satisfying

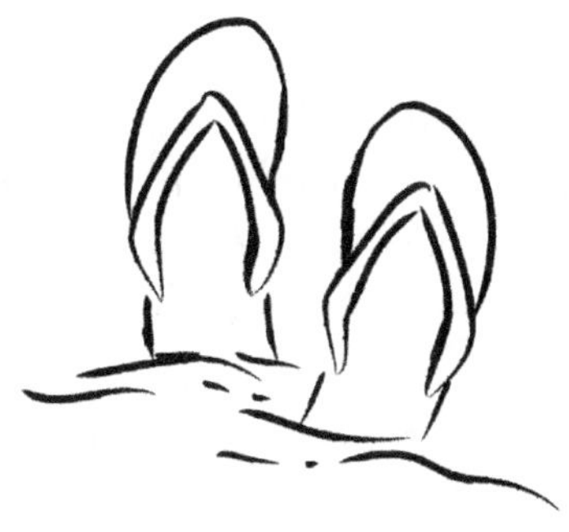

What is love?

But what is love if not a state of connection, a moment of joy, a wondrous glimpse into an infinite world of hope bedazzled by the euphoric outpouring of emotion?

But what is love if not a life of joy and sadness, pleasure and pain, a sentimental longing for a time that has passed, an experience that bonds us through memories, memories that become immortalised, transcribed from one generation to the next?

But what is love if not the sense of belonging, a secret glance, a stolen kiss, a passionate embrace, a smile that sets free the encapsulated soul, a rush of excitement enmeshed with intangible emotions?

But what is love if not the capacity to feel that which cannot be felt without the unbearable searing pain of heartbreak or a hunger for a touch that will never be felt again?

But what is love if it is not what we are here for?

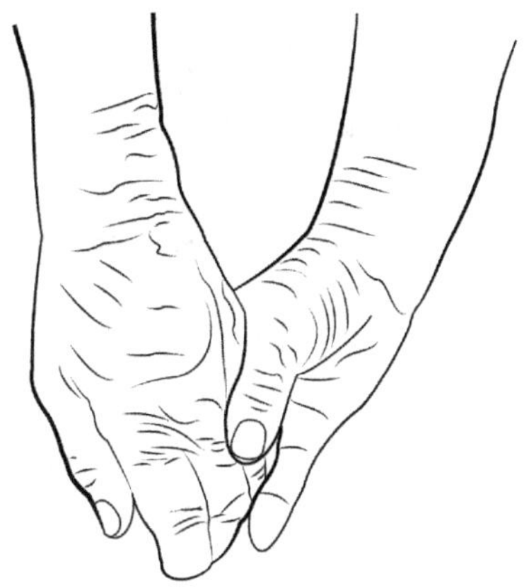

You never knew me

You never knew me like I thought you did.
I was your friend

Whatever it is that friendship means.

Perception is a funny thing
I perceived we were friends

Shared secrets, shared dreams
Too intertwined. Not separate.

Too selfish to see the friend you had in me
I was not there to blame
I was not there to take sides

I was there to share what I had inside
And what I had was love

I messed up a time or two, but let's be honest, so
did you.
Forgiveness blurred but honouring time.

Time spent as friends, too interwind. Not
separate

I ignored the way you looked at me.
I did not believe you could believe that of me.

It was not true. You never knew me.

When love finds you

Love finds you patient.
It finds you when you can forgive.

He will understand all of you.
He will make you laugh.

You will laugh together.

Love finds you letting go
It finds you when you can see.

She will understand all of you
She will make you laugh

You will laugh together.

It will be ok
Because love will be there forever.